The One Things

The One Things

A Heartwarming Story About What's Most Important

Dr. C. Todd Fetter

Xulon Press

Xulon Press
2301 Lucien Way #415
Maitland, FL 32751
407.339.4217
www.xulonpress.com

© 2017 by Dr. C. Todd Fetter

Printed in the United States of America.
Edited by Xulon Press.

Illustrated by Caleb Grace

ISBN-13: 9781545619674

DEDICATION

To my daughter Victoria who never ceases to amaze me with her strong and determined pursuit of life. One of the greatest joys I've ever known is the privilege of being your dad. Thank you for always making others feel important and loved. The way in which you live is truly an inspiration. I smile every time I think of you.

TABLE OF CONTENTS

CHAPTER 1

Grandpa Ed lived most of his life wondering what it would have been like to be a father. He always loved to be around children because of their unending sense of wonder and curiosity. Grandpa Ed, as he was most affectionately called, thought his nickname was rather strange since he didn't, in fact, have any children of his own.

He likely got his nickname from being the kindest man in the entire town. People loved to hear Grandpa Ed tell of the wonders of life, full of daring and captivating adventures. He kept a great story ready for anyone willing to listen. He always made time for other people, especially children. This is how he made so many good friends. He knew what a good Grandpa was supposed to be like.

During the school year, Grandpa Ed awoke early every morning and walked to the school crossing to greet the children. He said in his hearty, robust voice, "Good morning kids! Hope you have a great day!"

His voice even sounded like a good grandpa. All the children waved and greeted him; some even ran to give him a hug.

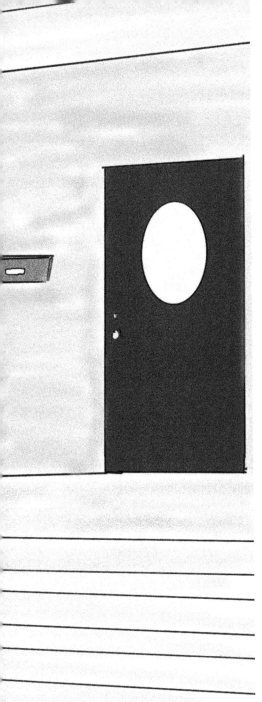

After school, the children who walked home made sure to pass by Grandpa Ed's house, hoping he was doing yard work or fixing something outside.

As soon as they saw him in his yard, they ran as fast as they could, eager to hear another amazing story. Grandpa Ed told every story with the most incredible detail. He delivered his tales with compelling passion. Everyone who heard them felt as if they were part of his story. He spoke of true events, usually describing his life as a missionary.

Grandpa Ed never married and had dedicated his life to helping orphaned children all around the world. He traveled to remote places where children were often neglected and many times left to take care of themselves. Telling stories to children made him feel useful and gave him continued purpose.

One day, during mid-summer, when kids in the neighborhood were outside playing, news spread that Grandpa Ed was sick and in the hospital.

Emma, a little girl who lived on the same street as Grandpa Ed asked her mom, "Will you take me and a few friends to the hospital to see Grandpa Ed?"

Emma's mom replied, "Sure, honey, we can go Saturday."

Emma stated, "No, Mom, we can't wait that long. That's four days away and he might not be there then."

Seeing how upset she was, Emma's mom finally said, "Okay, I'll take you and your friends first thing in the morning."

Emma said excitedly, "Thank you so much, Mom! I'm going to call the others and let them know."

CHAPTER 2

Early the next morning, the children were up and ready to go see Grandpa Ed even before their parents woke up!

Making a conference call on her phone, Emma instructed her friends saying, "Okay everyone, be at my house in thirty minutes."

They all agreed to meet at her house and ride together for their trip to see Grandpa Ed. Emma's mom had a big van they could all ride in together.

When all the children arrived at her house, Emma's mom was ready to go. Before heading to the car, she counted all the kids. She said, "Okay, let's see who we have with us today."

James spoke up, "I'm here!"

"Good morning, James," she replied.

Sophia, who lived just around the corner, said, "I brought some snacks for us, Mrs. Taylor."

"Why that's so sweet of you, Sophia. Thank you," she said.

"I'm ready to go," said Max.

"Good morning, Max."

Emma said, "Where's Noah? He's supposed to be here by now."

Just about the time Emma finished saying that, Noah came running around the end of the driveway yelling, "Hey! Don't leave without me, I'm coming!"

James started laughing and said, "Leave it to Noah to be late."

Emma's mom counted the children once again and said, "Okay, I believe everyone is here."

They all got in her van and drove to the hospital.

As soon as they arrived, the kids jumped out of the van and ran as fast as they could through the hospital's front door. They ran straight to the information desk and Emma said loudly, "Can you help us please? We're trying to find our friend! His name is Grandpa Ed!"

Noah blurted out, "Yeah, he's our best friend and we need to see him right away!"

A nurse gathered them together and said, "Children, please calm down. This is a hospital. It's just like school where you need to be quiet. Everyone take a deep breath."

The children took a deep breath just as they were told.

She continued, "Okay, now listen. I promise to take you to see your friend as soon as possible. Everyone follow me to the waiting area while I make sure your friend is ready for a visit. You can sit here and watch the television until I come back."

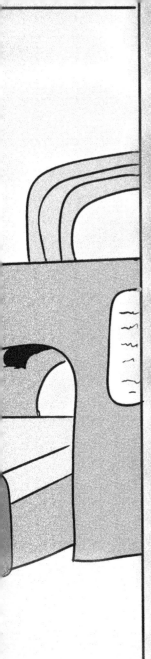

The children sat down and looked around the room.

Noah said, "Look, guys, Batman is on TV. Let's watch."

Max and James joined him.

Sophia whispered to Emma, "I sure hope Grandpa Ed is okay."

Emma replied, "Me too. I'm so worried about him."

After about twenty minutes, James said, "Man, how long is this going to take? It's feels like we've been waiting for hours."

Just then the nurse entered and said, "Okay children, we can go now."

They got up immediately, forming a little huddle group as they walked and followed the nurse.

They walked together down several hallways and got onto an elevator, which took them to the floor where Grandpa Ed was staying.

Exiting the elevator, they huddled closer, when Max asked, "What kind of hospital are we in? I've never seen equipment like this."

Sophia replied, "Oh, it'll be okay, Max. Just keep close and don't touch anything."

They continued following the nurse until they arrived at another hallway that revealed a big see-through door at the end.

As they walked slowly toward the big door, the nurse pushed a button on the wall and it opened.

Taking a few steps in, she said, "You have some visitors who are anxious to see you, sir."

That's when they heard a familiar, but somewhat softer, voice call out, "Well, send them on in!"

As the children entered the room still tightly huddled together, Grandpa Ed looked at them goofily and asked, "Are y'all cold or something? Why are you huddled up like that?"

The children looked at each other.

Emma laughed and said, "Wow, we must have looked pretty stupid walking around like this."

The nurse laughed and before leaving them said, "Now if any y'all kids need blankets to keep warm, just let me know."

Grandpa Ed must have thought her comment was funny because he let out a snort that made the whole situation even funnier. All the kids and Grandpa Ed laughed so hard, it hurt. One boy even cried, he laughed so much.

Emma, the self-proclaimed leader of the group, spoke up and asked Grandpa Ed, "What are you doing in the hospital? What happened to you?"

Grandpa Ed smiled wide, held his arms toward the children, and said, "Come on in, kids, and give your old friend a hug."

They all did.

When the hugs were finished, Grandpa Ed said, in the gentlest tone, "Children, Grandpa Ed has a few problems with his heart. But don't you worry, everything will be all right. Do you understand?"

Max whispered to James, "What does he mean by 'a few problems with his heart'?"

"What's wrong with your heart, dude?" James blurted out.

Suddenly there was a hush in the room and everyone was as still as a mouse.

Concerned about them knowing the truth, Grandpa Ed said, "It's nothing, just a checkup. There's no reason to be upset."

Fighting back a few tears, he continued, "Who wants to hear another story?"

James yelled, "Now that's what I'm talking about!"

Sitting up, Grandpa Ed instructed, "Okay kids, get up on the bed and get comfortable. I've been saving this one for awhile."

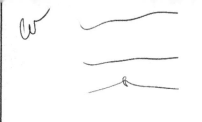

CHAPTER 3

The children crawled onto the bed—everyone except Sophia. She was too busy looking at all the medical equipment and trying to read the nurses' whiteboard. Sophia wanted to be a nurse when she grew up.

As the others sat on the bed, waiting for Grandpa Ed to speak, the nurse walked in.

Sophia's attention was transferred immediately to her and she asked, "Hey! What does this machine do? What does that word mean? What does that beeping sound mean? How long have you been a nurse?" Sophia asked questions so fast, the nurse didn't have time to answer a single one.

The nurse was not happy seeing the kids on the bed and sternly said, "You kids get down off that bed right now!"

Grandpa Ed held a hand toward her and softly said, "It's okay. Leave them alone. I asked them to get up here with me. Just do what you came in here to do and we'll be all right."

The nurse nodded her head and quietly put some things on the counter by the sink and made a few marks on her whiteboard. Sophia watched her every move.

Sophia was still asking questions when the nurse turned to her and said, "Honey, you need to stop asking me so many questions and join your friends."

Sophia replied, "Well I'm going to be a nurse one day too and I want to know everything I can about being a nurse. I'm going to take care of everyone!"

All she could say in response to Sophia was, "Yes ma'am, I believe you will."

Recognizing that Sophia was taking it all in, she asked, "Honey, would you like to help me?"

"Of course!" Sophia exclaimed. "I'm excited to do anything that requires nursing skills."

"Okay then, write these numbers down on this piece of paper. I also need you to wipe down the sink and countertops; here's a cloth and some cleaning spray."

Sophia said, "Oh, I'm so excited."

The nurse, confident her little co-worker would keep busy, closed the door as she left the room.

The other kids had been watching the nurse and Sophia. They looked back at Grandpa Ed as he called, "Sophia, come join the others."

She answered, "Not right now, Grandpa Ed. I'm too busy doing nurse stuff."

He didn't say anything. He just looked at them, one by one.

He noticed their clothes and he noticed their hair. He looked at their shoes and if they had socks on or not. He even took each one by the hand, looking to see if their fingernails were clean.

Grandpa Ed had always told the children that cleanliness was next to godliness and they believed him.

Grandpa Ed said, "I love you guys from the bottom of my heart. Your kind words and attention has meant the world to me."

Emma started to cry and said, "Grandpa Ed, I don't want you to die."

Grandpa Ed wiped a tear from her cheek and said, "Nope, none of that today, okay? I'm not going anywhere. I just have to get checked out, that's all."

With that bit of encouragement, Emma was able to smile again.

Noah said, "Well, I think we can all feel better now."

Grandpa Ed reached over and grabbed Noah by the ear and asked, "Noah, why do you always wear that hat, son? I don't ever think I've seen you without it."

Noah dropped his head and replied while shrugging his shoulders, "Uh, I don't know, just like it I guess."

Grandpa Ed laughed and said, "Well, a fine cap it is. It suits you, Noah. I like it even though it could use a good rinsin' next time you wash your fingernails."

Laughter again filled the hospital room and Noah said, "Sure thing, Grandpa Ed."

He called out to Sophia once more, who by this time, was cleaning the countertops across the room. Grandpa Ed asked her, "Sophia, why don't you put that down and come over here with us?"

Sophia never looked up, but continued her cleaning. It was clear she wasn't paying attention.

After taking a deep breath and exhaling slowly, Grandpa Ed said, "Kids, listen to me. I'm going to share a story with you; one I've never shared with anyone else. Will that be okay?"

"Sure!" exclaimed the children.

"Let's hear it," said James.

"Yes, yes!" replied Emma.

The children settled in, making sure they were comfortable enough to listen for a long time.

CHAPTER 4

When Grandpa Ed saw that they were ready and had their full attention, he began.

"Each one of you," he said, "has unique talents and abilities that I've not seen in any other children."

The children looked at each other.

Grandpa Ed continued, "I'm about to share with you the most wonderful story I've ever had the privilege of tellin' anyone. I've been waitin' on the perfect time, and now is just about the most perfect time there will ever be, so y'all take a look at one of your hands. Go ahead now; take a good look."

Each child raised a hand and looked at it, exactly as Grandpa Ed asked. Looking at their hands, they said altogether, "Now what?"

Grandpa Ed chuckled and asked the children, "Okay, now how many fingers do you have on one hand?"

Each of them replied, "Five!"

"That's right," said Grandpa Ed. "Each one of your fingers will represent an important lesson I'm about to explain to you. Got it?"

"We got it," said Noah.

Sophia, though still cleaning, acknowledged Grandpa Ed's question by raising an open hand letting him know she was listening.

Grandpa Ed, now looking serious, said, "Each one of your fingers is just one thing that I want you to learn. Since we have five fingers, there's gonna be five one things."

James said, "I'm not sure what you mean, but I trust you, Grandpa Ed."

The other children nodded.

Chapter 5

Grandpa Ed started by asking them to take a look at their thumbs. Directing his attention to Emma, Grandpa Ed said, "You've always been the most curious child. You've always asked a lot of questions which is a good thing because it means you're always learnin'."

Grandpa Ed thought for a moment and continued, "A very wise man once said, 'if anyone asks a question, he is a fool for five minutes. He who does not ask a question remains a fool forever.'"

Emma spoke up and said, "Wow, my dad tells me the exact same thing all the time!"

After giving her a big smile, Grandpa Ed said, "I'm going to tell you about one of my favorite stories. It's about a little shepherd boy who lived in a far away land. This boy's childhood was much like your own and through normal, everyday experiences, he learned many important things."

Grandpa Ed asked, "Before I continue, do you remember what I've always made a habit to say?"

"Oh, yes sir," said Noah. "You always say we just need to have eyes that can see and ears that can hear."

"That's right," Grandpa Ed commended.

Continuing, he said, "This young boy was born into a large family and grew up the youngest of eight brothers. As he grew and obeyed his parents, he was allowed to do important chores. One in which he was good at was being a shepherd. He took good care of the family's sheep, keeping them safe and making sure they all got home at the end of the day. As this young boy grew older, a wise prophet came to where he lived. He came to announce a new king over the land. Can any of you guess what he did?"

The children shrugged.

"The old prophet said this young shepherd boy was going to be the next king! Can you imagine that?"

"Here this boy is, only about twelve years old, and he is going to be the next king! Why, that's not much older than some of you are now."

The children squirmed with excitement as they normally did when Grandpa Ed compared his story's characters with them.

"He must have been a special child," said Grandpa Ed. "And do you know why I think that?"

Again, the children shrugged.

Looking straight at Emma, Grandpa Ed said, "I believe he was a special child because he liked to ask good questions."

Emma's eyes brightened at his statement.

Grandpa Ed said, "This young boy finally did become king. Emma, this young boy learned a lot by asking questions but the most important thing he ever asked was this..."

Picking up his Bible, Grandpa Ed turned its pages and read, *"I ask only one thing from the Lord. This is what I want most: Let me live in the Lord's house all my life, enjoying the Lord's beauty and spending time in his palace'"* (Psalm 27:4).

"You see kids," Grandpa Ed said, "whenever you look at your thumb, you need to remember to ask the right questions and you will be honored like the young shepherd boy who became king. God even said he was a person after His own heart."

Grandpa Ed added, "It would make my heart feel so much better if y'all would always remember that."

Emma said loudly, "Well if it'll make your heart better, I'll never forget it. I promise Grandpa Ed!"

The other kids shouted, "Me too, me too!"

Grandpa Ed noticed he did feel better after hearing them say that.

The nurse must have heard them shout as she quickly came in to check on her patient. She walked over to the stand by Grandpa Ed's bed and noticed right away that his blood pressure had improved quite a bit.

She wrote some numbers on a pad, turned around and said, "Well, whatever y'all talking about must be good, so keep it up."

Turning to her patient, she asked, "Do you need anything for pain or something to make you more comfortable?"

He smiled and said, "No ma'am, I believe I've got all I need right here, but thanks."

The nurse left again and the children waited until the big door shut before turning back to their friend, when Noah inquired, "Okay, what's next?"

Grandpa Ed smiled at Noah and replied, "Noah, I'm glad you asked."

CHAPTER 6

Focusing on his hand, Grandpa Ed said, "Now let's take a look at our index fingers, the ones we point with." So all the children held up their pointer fingers and waited for what he was going to say next.

"This finger," said Grandpa Ed, "is the second one thing I want you to remember. It represents all the stuff we have and all the things we want. We usually use this finger to point to all of those things, right?"

The children nodded.

Grandpa Ed looked toward Noah, who was peering out from under his cap.

"Noah," said Grandpa Ed, "I want to direct this next one thing to you. From all the children I've come to know and love, you're one of the most interesting kids I've ever met."

Noah held his head up a little and smiled.

Grandpa Ed continued, "Noah, my young friend, I've watched you for many years. I remember you being one of the first kids in our neighborhood to have a bicycle. I have thoroughly enjoyed just how well you mastered the skill of riding a bicycle. I remember when you first got it. You weren't too good, were you?"

Noah laughed and replied, "Nope, but I got better!"

Grandpa Ed laughed too and said, "Yes, yes you did, my boy. You got better almost overnight. As I recall, your bicycle was the newest and shiniest bicycle on the block too. You had the best bicycle, a new helmet, new elbow pads, knee pads, and yes, I do believe you even had a fancy gear shifter, am I right?"

"Oh yeah, it was the best bike money could buy, Grandpa Ed!" Noah responded.

Grandpa Ed just smiled at him.

"Noah," Grandpa Ed said, "I want you to also know I watched how you treated your friends concerning that new bicycle. I remember many times when you wouldn't share and let the kids who didn't have a bicycle ride your bike when they asked. You certainly didn't have to, but you sure could have, don't ya think?"

Noah lowered his head.

"I also remember when you showed off a new backpack and made fun of some of the other kids who didn't have one," Grandpa Ed said.

By this time, Noah had lowered his head even more.

Without looking up, he said, "I don't like the way this story is going, Grandpa Ed."

"I'm sure you don't Noah, but there is a powerful lesson in this if you'll allow me to continue."

Noah sighed and said, "Sure, Grandpa Ed, go ahead."

"Noah," said Grandpa Ed, "You remind me of a man who lived long ago who had everything life could offer. He had many horses and cattle, sheep, and all the animals anyone could ever want. He lived in a big house with all the stuff everyone else wanted, but couldn't afford. He was rich beyond measure. He had it all, or so he thought. This man thought having a lot of things would make him happy. What he didn't realize was he was missing the most important one thing. There was one thing that he didn't have. Do you know what it was, Noah?"

Noah shrugged and said, "Nope. What was he missing, Grandpa Ed?"

"He was missing the one thing that we all need and that is putting our trust and hope in Jesus, rather than putting our trust and hope in all the stuff we think will make us happy," Grandpa Ed explained.

"This man who owned just about everything can also be found in the Bible. Long story short, he met Jesus one day. This is what he said to him:

'Jesus looked at the man in a way that showed how much he cared for him. He said, "There is still one thing you need to do. Go and sell everything you have. Give the money to those who are poor, and you will have riches in heaven. Then come and follow me." The man was upset when Jesus told him to give away his money. He didn't want to do this, because he was very rich. So he went away sad.' (Mark 10:21-22)

"This man put his trust and hopes in all his things. What we need to know is having Jesus in our lives is the greatest thing we could ever hope to have. He's more important than our toys, our houses, even our families, everything!"

The room was so quiet, you could have heard a pin drop.

Grandpa Ed interrupted the silence and said, "When you have Jesus, turns out you have everything, even if you don't have a shiny new bicycle because Jesus owns it all anyway."

Noah perked up and asked, "So if I trust Jesus first then He'll give me everything I need, right?"

Astonished, Grandpa Ed remarked, "Noah, how did you know that? That's exactly right, son! It's important to understand Jesus will provide everything we need, not everything we want. Where did you come up with that, Noah?"

"Oh I heard it in Sunday School. I don't know a lot, but I'm a good listener!" Noah answered.

"Well, my son," said Grandpa Ed, "You are without a doubt a most peculiar child. Now let's see you put some of that wisdom into practice, eh?"

"Sure thing," Noah replied, "I was already thinking about giving my bicycle to Max since he doesn't have one. I can probably get another one anyway."

Noah noticed the amazed look on the others' faces and said, "And you know what else? I bet my dad would allow me to sell some of my stuff to help some other kids who don't have much. That way we could all have something!"

After hearing this, a tear fell down Grandpa Ed's cheek. He and the rest of the kids sat surprised by what Noah had said.

Max reached out and gave him a fist bump and said, "Dude, are you sure? That's the nicest thing anyone has ever done for me. Thanks!"

Noah returned his fist bump and said, "Yeah, I'm sure. That's what buddies are for."

Grandpa Ed cleared his throat and said, "Well, I do believe this story is going to be better than I expected."

Chapter 7

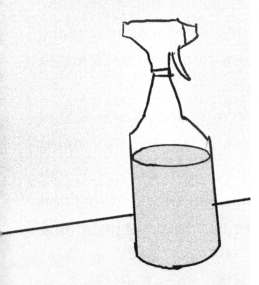

By this time, little Sophia had just about cleaned everything in the room as far up the walls as she could reach.

Grandpa Ed spoke to her, in a firm but loving tone, "Sophia, the next one thing is for you. Please join us."

Sophia stopped, turned to him and asked, "Grandpa Ed, can't I just keep doing what I'm doing? It's important work because I'm helping keep this place clean so you can get better."

Humbled, Grandpa Ed said, "Sophia, thank you for working so hard but it's time to join us now. That would make me feel better."

Sophia laid her cleaning cloth down, jumped up on the bed with the others, and said, "Okay, I'm ready."

Grandpa Ed, nodding his head, said, "All righty then, here we go."

"Sophia," he said, "You are without a doubt the busiest little girl I've ever known. Since we first met, you've always made sure everyone else is okay, making sure everything is just right."

"It's my job," said Sophia. "I like helping and making sure everyone is taken care of."

"And you do it so well," responded Grandpa Ed.

"Well, my momma tells me that keeping busy keeps me out of trouble and that I'm supposed to help others whenever I can," said Sophia.

Grandpa Ed replied, "And you have a wise momma for telling you that. What I want to share with you, dear, is that keeping busy is a great thing, especially when taking care of others. You have been given an excellent gift and I'm proud you recognize it at such an early age."

"Sophia," he continued, "you are a special child with the unique ability to put others first. I admire that about you the most. A gift such as yours is wonderful, but be careful with it. The truth about your gift is that you can become so busy doing things for others that you miss the one thing that you need. This one thing is to be focused on the best thing instead of just doing a good thing."

"Can you really see that in me?" Sophia asked.

"Sophia, my sweet child, you remind me of another story about a woman who had the same gift as you. Her story is found in the Bible too."

Turning the pages of his Bible, Grandpa Ed found the passage. "Here it is," he said. "'But the Lord answered her, "Martha, Martha, you are getting worried and upset about too many things. Only one thing is important. Mary has made the right choice, and it will never be taken away from her."' (Luke 10:41–42)

"She always made sure people were taken care of and kept her house clean. She made sure there was plenty of food for people to eat when they came by for a visit. One day, an important man came to visit her home. She knew this visitor was a special person, so she ordered her family to help make everything perfect. As the visitor began talking, this woman couldn't stop working long enough to hear what he was saying, even though she wanted to."

Sophia interrupted and said, "That's how I felt too. I wanted to hear what you were saying, Grandpa Ed, but I wanted you to feel better even more."

Grandpa Ed replied, "Yes, I know you did." He continued, "This lady got upset at her sister because she had stopped working to listen to this man instead of helping. The visitor noticed how upset she was so he stopped and explained to her that while serving others is good, it was more important to listen to what he was saying."

Sophia said, "Wow. I got a little carried away, didn't I?"

"Sophia, I'm telling you to be careful of being so busy for others that you miss what is meant for you," Grandpa Ed replied.

"I think I get it," Sophia said. "It means that I can get so busy that I end up missing something important, right?"

"Yes, that's it!" Grandpa Ed remarked.

Sophia turned to Emma and said, "I'm sorry, Emma."

"Sorry for what?" asked Emma.

"You didn't know it, but I was upset with you for not getting down and helping me clean the room for Grandpa Ed.

"It's not your fault," she continued. "I just got carried away and thought it was my job to do something good for someone I cared about. I realize now that the best place I could have been was up here with my friends and sharing time with Grandpa Ed."

Sophia and Emma gave each other a great big hug.

"Well, I believe everything's going to be all right, children," said Grandpa Ed. "I think everyone is where they ought to be and that's what matters now."

Chapter 8

Grandpa Ed looked at the remaining two children, James and Max. He thought for a moment and said, "Max, I believe your story has already been told and will be the fourth one thing I'm going to share."

Max looked up and asked, "Uh, what do you mean, Grandpa Ed?"

"What I mean, Max," Grandpa Ed said, "Is this: how did you feel when you heard Noah was going to give you his bicycle?"

"Well, uh, kind of surprised at first, you know?"

"Yes, I thought you may have felt that way," Grandpa Ed said. "Why did you feel surprised, Max?"

"Well I guess I felt like Noah has everything a kid could ever want, and I don't have much at all," answered Max.

Grandpa Ed asked, "Do you feel this way often, Max?"

Max answered, "Uh, I don't know, I just feel sad and left out sometimes."

"Well I'm sure you do," replied Grandpa Ed. "Sometimes when we look at others and see all that they have compared to the little we might have, it can make us feel a little weird inside."

"Yep," answered Max, "That's how I feel–a little weird."

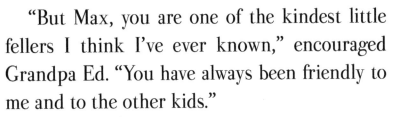

"But Max, you are one of the kindest little fellers I think I've ever known," encouraged Grandpa Ed. "You have always been friendly to me and to the other kids."

"Yes sir; my mom and dad told me to always be nice to other people even when they aren't so nice to me," said Max. "I've always felt like I didn't fit in because I don't have much stuff like other kids. I'm a nice guy, but I'm usually quiet around others. A lot of times I don't think other people even notice me."

"I often wondered why you were the quiet one," stated Grandpa Ed. "Well, Max, what do you think of Noah and his gift now?"

Max smiled as he said, "It's the greatest thing anyone has ever done for me! Thanks again, Noah!"

Max thought about giving Noah a big hug too, but decided a high five would be better since they were guys.

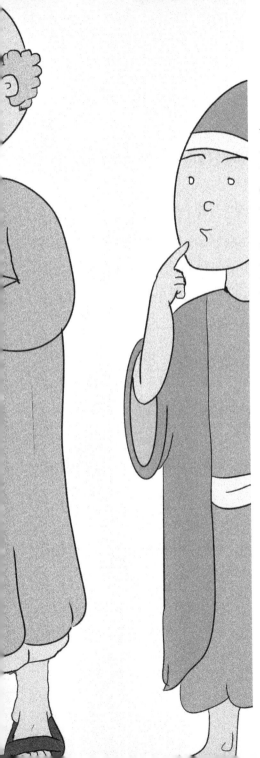

Grandpa Ed said, "Max, I want to share with you a story about a man who was blind. He couldn't see anything. He loved people, but couldn't participate in activities with them because of his blindness. He sometimes felt as if other people were blind too because they acted like they couldn't see him either. This made the blind man sad and lonely until one day, a great man came to the town where he lived. This great man walked up to where he was and started talking to him. They had a good talk about different things going in the city and after some time, the great man asked the blind man if he wanted to see.

"The blind man answered, 'Oh yes, more than anything!'

"So the great man leaned over and, using his fingers, touched the man's eyes and said, 'You can now see.'

"Immediately, the man saw everything! He had been healed of his blindness because of the kindness and power of the great man. He jumped up and ran all over town, telling everyone about the miracle that had taken place. Many of the people recognized him as the blind man and marveled. When asked about his condition, *He replied, 'One thing I do know. I was blind but now I see!'"*

Grandpa Ed said, "Max, the man didn't use fancy words or study a long time to tell what had happened to him. It wasn't important that he was poor and couldn't do what other people could do. He simply told what he knew was the truth, and from those simple words, everyone who heard them was amazed."

Grandpa Ed leaned toward Max and said, "So, Max, do you understand the lesson in this story?"

"Yeah, I think so," Max replied. "All I know is I didn't have a bike, but now I do!"

The children and Grandpa Ed laughed and fell back onto the bed, giggling at such a funny, but true, comment.

"Yes, I believe you understand just fine," Grandpa Ed said.

Holding up his Bible, Grandpa Ed said, "You can read all about this blind man in this wonderful book."

After being quiet for a moment, James spoke up and said, "Grandpa Ed, is there anything you'd like to tell me?"

CHAPTER 9

Grandpa Ed sat up and replied, "Yes, James, there certainly is. Pay attention because this part of the story is also important. It's going to be the fifth one thing that I want you to know."

They all sat up, excited to hear what Grandpa Ed was going to say next.

Grandpa Ed said, "James, my young friend, I've known you the longest time of all the children in the neighborhood. What I have seen from you, sir, is that you are a determined young boy."

James inquired, "What's that supposed to mean?"

Grandpa Ed, putting his hand on James' shoulder, said, "It means you always want to finish everything you start. I've seen how you approach every challenge you face. Regardless of how difficult the task, you never give up. That's called determination."

"Oh, yes sir; my daddy says I got somethin' called 'the fight' in me; says I got it from my Grampy Johnson. He was a real life prize fighter."

"I've heard of him," answered Grandpa Ed. "He was a great one, too. I remember one of his most famous boxing matches where he went the distance and fought for twelve hard rounds. Everyone thought he should have quit in the fourth round, but he kept on fightin', and eventually won the match. James, I suppose your father is right in saying you got your determination from your Grandpa."

James sat up a little higher, feeling proud of his Grampy Johnson.

In a more serious tone, Grandpa Ed said, "James, I remember the day when the new playground opened at the city park and how excited you were."

Sophia perked up and said, "Yep, my dad was chairman of the park committee then."

"Yes, I do believe you are right, Sophia," said Grandpa Ed. "And what a wonderful job he did, too."

Grandpa Ed said to James, "Son, I remember what happened to you the first day it opened. You remember too, don't you?"

James, looking surprised said, "Yes sir, I remember."

"Care to remind us what happened that day, James?" Grandpa Ed asked.

James replied, "Well, sure Grandpa Ed, I guess so."

"Please tell us, James," said Emma. "I don't remember what happened."

"Okay," uttered James. "I remember waking up early because I wanted to be the first kid to climb the rope net and write my name at the top of the pole. I wanted my name to be the first one there so everyone would know 'James Johnson' was first."

James didn't say anything else.

Emma asked, "Well, James, what happened? What happened when you reached the top?"

James answered, "Nothin' happened 'cause I didn't make it to the top."

"What? What happened, James?" she inquired.

"Well, I was in such a hurry to get to the park I forgot my climbing gloves and decided to climb without them. About half way up, my hands were sweating so much, I lost my grip and fell to the ground," James explained.

Emma responded, "Oh no! James, did you get hurt?"

James quietly sat with his head down.

Grandpa Ed softly said, "James, it's okay, son. Take your time and face it. When you're ready, tell us what happened."

James took a deep breath and said, "Well, I landed in an awkward position and did this."

He slowly held up his right hand to reveal a crooked little pinkie finger.

Emma gasped, "Oh my! Does it hurt?"

"Yeah it hurt like the dickens then, but it's okay now. I just have a crooked little finger, that's all."

Grandpa Ed said, "Now James, I saved this story for last because you model perfectly the lesson we can learn from the fifth one thing. You remind me of a smart man who lived a long time ago. He came to understand his life was headed in the wrong direction fast, kind of like you did when you fell from the rope net. This man had a dramatic encounter one day. He was always in a hurry to do the things he thought were good. He soon discovered he was actually doing bad things, so he decided to change his life right then and there. He made sure from then on to slow down and think about what he wanted to do. In this way, he could be certain all the things he did would benefit others."

James asked, "Well, how did he do that, Grandpa Ed?"

"He simply used the same determination he always used. Only now, he made sure that what he was doing would be good for everyone," Grandpa Ed explained. "He still had the same quality of being a hard worker and he used his gift of ambition to change his life and those around him. His story is in the Bible as well."

Turning the pages of his Bible, Grandpa Ed said, "This is what the man said about himself: *Brothers and sisters, I know that I still have a long way to go. But there is one thing I do: I forget what is in the past and try as*

hard as I can to reach the goal before me.'" (Philippians 3:13-14)

Grandpa Ed extended his arms and said, "You see, kids, this man didn't let his past failures define his future. He stayed focused. He learned what was most important and he wasn't going to back down. This man went on to be one of the greatest men who ever lived."

The children sat perfectly still, hanging on every word that Grandpa Ed spoke. Grandpa Ed knew he had once again captured their sense of wonder.

Letting the children think about what he shared, he finally said, "I believe it's time for a recap. Let's all hold up a hand with our fingers stretched out and see if we can remember what they stand for."

Chapter 10

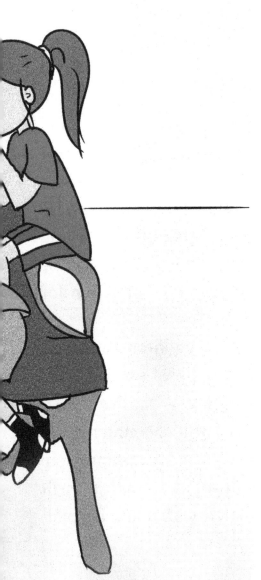

As each child held an open hand in the air, Grandpa Ed wiggled his thumb and said, "Emma, you remind me of King David, who learned the most important thing was searching for answers and knowing God is at the heart of prayer. He learned by asking good questions, and God honored him for it."

He wiggled his index finger, turned to Noah, and said, "Noah, you remind me of the rich young ruler who learned that knowing God is at the heart of surrender. Unlike him, when we can give out of love, it releases a special bond between those involved. Please keep your heart surrendered to the Lord and always remember that the most important things aren't things."

Wiggling his middle finger and looking at Sophia, Grandpa Ed continued, "Sweet Sophia, you remind me of Martha who kept busy doing all the things she thought made other people happy. She learned that knowing God is at the heart of service. Keep doing good things for others, but be certain you make time for yourself."

Wiggling his ring finger, Grandpa Ed winked and said, "Max, you remind me of the blind man who received his sight from the Lord. He learned that knowing God is at the heart of trust. Be bold to ask for what you need and always look for the good in others. In this way you will become a great promoter of compassion to those in need."

Finally, Grandpa Ed wiggled his pinkie finger and smiled at James. He said, "James, you remind me of the Apostle Paul, who learned that knowing God is at the heart of ambition. Your strong desire to finish a task will be rewarding. Just be sure to count the cost and use your determination for good things. In this way, you will be able to bless many."

Grandpa Ed took a deep breath while looking at the children with their hands lifted and said, "Children, this is the way it should be. Live your lives open-handed and remember what each finger represents. What I've shared with you is a story about staying focused. In life, you will encounter many things that will require hope, money, service, trust, and determination. Learn the lesson of the one things while you are still young so that you will remember them when you are older. The truths shared with you today will help keep you focused on what's most important."

"And that's our relationship with Jesus, right Grandpa Ed?" asked Emma.

"That's it, precisely! You are such a smart girl!

"Always study hard and learn to know God. He carefully created you and has given each of you special talents and gifts. He expects you to develop them and use them for good. If you will do this with the right purpose in your heart, you will experience the greatest joy you could ever know. Knowing God through the one things is to know what's most important."

All the children smiled at Grandpa Ed, and he smiled back at them. The hospital room was filled with true love. They all knew it and felt it.

Grandpa Ed yawned and said, "My dear little ones, I think it's time for you to go now. I'm tired and I need to rest. Thank you for coming to see me and for being good listeners. You are all such good kids and you have made me feel so much better."

The kids got down off of the bed and gave Grandpa Ed a kiss, a high five, or a fist bump and silently walked out of the room.

As the last child left and the big door closed behind them, Grandpa Ed looked over at the heart monitor, sighed a little, grinned, and fell fast asleep...

Acknowledgments

I would like to extend first and foremost gratitude to the Father who, through his Holy Spirit, encouraged the idea for this book. Your Truth is everlasting.

A special thanks to my wife Chere' who graciously listened to me throughout this process. Your kindness is always refreshing.

Thanks to Pastor Adam Hicks, one of the most compelling people I know who never fails to extend genuine concern to all he encounters.

To all who selflessly gave their time in praying, reading, editing and offering criticism, both kind and otherwise. Many thanks go to Lonnie Ingle, Kelli Lacy, Linda Silas, Margaret Myrick, Erin Wright and Dr. Ken Anderson. This book is so much better for having your input. Your friendship is cherished.

To Caleb Grace who illustrated this book. You are one of the smartest and talented illustrators I have ever worked with. I appreciate the fine gift God has given you.

Thanks to Desperation Church. Your love of God is contagious! Thank you for allowing His light to shine so brightly in your lives.

Special Acknowledgement

Inspiration for this book was taken from the writing of Mr. Camden McAfee. He is communication coordinator at PULSE, an evangelistic ministry that exists to awaken culture to the reality of Jesus. He writes about knowing God at Countercultural.

CPSIA information can be obtained
at www.ICGtesting.com
Printed in the USA
LVHW02s2322180118
562756LV00001B/1/P